The Chiropractor's guide to Direct-Response Marketing

Make every mailing profitable!

By Fritz Richard

Introduction

Wouldn't marketing and advertising be great if you could consistently get excellent results?

Most marketing campaigns are hit or miss — with many, unfortunately, being a "miss." Direct-response marketing, however, is designed to do one thing: Get customers now! And unlike most other marketing efforts, direct marketing is designed to get quantifiable results — results you can see, feel, and count.

Imagine being able to choose how many new patients you wish to obtain each month. Increase your business as fast or as slowly as you want — that's the power of effective, consistent, direct-mail marketing.

Fortunately, there are foundational principles for creating a lucrative direct-response campaign, and if followed properly, every mailing can be profitable.

Successful steps to follow

Step 1: Why are you special? Research key attributes of your practice and find out what makes your practice the best in town. You can even ask some of your patients what they like about your service and what made them choose you over all the other chiropractors. After asking 20 to 40 of them you should see a pattern emerge.

If most of them say, "you really care," you can use that as your unique selling proposition (USP). More than likely, there will be many other reasons they like your practice, but let's say for example's sake that is the main reason.

Step 2: Say it in a tagline. If you don't have a tagline, create one. You could go with something such as, "We feel better, when you feel better," to connect with your USP, and you should use it as often as possible.

Step 3: Headline power! This is where most direct-response campaigns mess up. The headline is the first thing patients see when they open the letter, and it can make or break your response rate. Sometimes it's the only thing they read before deciding to throw it in the trash, so you need to make it a great one.

Your headline has to get the prospective patient to want to read the letter. It has to hit them hard and it has to hit them fast. For the most part, if you talk about the main benefits of your practice, you'll be OK.

After you come up with a solid headline, add a subheadline underneath it. This reinforces the main headline.

For example: The main headline is, "Feel 10 years younger," the subhead could be, "In only 30 minutes time." Or, if the main headline is, "Your health is our business," the subhead could be, "And we've been healing patients for 15 years."

Step 4: Body of evidence. Now that you have a great tagline, headline, and subheadline, let's add some effective body copy. Here's the key to good body copy: Keep it interesting.

Give the person a good reason to keep reading. The more they read the more patients you'll get. It's a proven fact, long copy gets more response. So if you can write a four page letter that gets read, you'll get a very good response from your direct-response mailing campaign. Remember, start new paragraphs with subheads to entice the reader.

Step 5: The postscript. Add a great "P.S." to the end of your letter. Many readers (45 percent) scan the body of the letter and read the P.S. before reading the whole letter. And don't forget to ask them to take some kind of action, whether it's make a call to your office, send in a response card, or send you an e-mail address.

Step 6: Hit the target. Find a good target market to mail to — the more specific the better. Some categories you may want to consider are the "Over 50" crowd, martial artists, manual laborers, etc. Whichever group you choose, make sure the letter's copy is directed toward their needs.

The Final Step: Get it opened! After you've done a great job creating this persuasive direct-response piece, make sure it gets opened. More than 92 percent of all unsolicited mail is never opened.

To make sure yours is open almost every time, you can:

- Hand address each letter. Some companies offer this as a service and it can cost about one dollar per letter including postage.

- Use a "live" stamp, not a bulk rate logo printed on the envelope.

- Not print a company logo or name on the envelope, just the return address.

These get more than 98 percent of letters opened just about every time.

It is important to know what causes a direct-mail campaign to fail, and how to prevent it from happening to you.

The most cause for failure is the lack of customer research — knowing who they are and exactly what they want — but you can prevent this by performing extensive market research before creating a direct-mail campaign.

Be specific about who you are hoping to reach with your message, and success can be yours.

LET'S TALK NUMBERS

A local mailing of 3,000 will result in a .05 percent to 2 percent response rate. In real numbers, you can expect between 15 and 60 prospective new clients. This will cost on average $1,700 if you produce the mailing yourself ($3,000 to have a service do it).

A monthly investment of $1,700 is a hefty investment, but the real question is how much is 15 new clients worth to your business?

In the worse case scenario, you will only gain seven new clients from each mailing. If your new client visits twice a year on average, and the cost per visit is $60 per visit, each new client is worth $120 per year. Seven new clients will bring in $840 the first year.

Each practice will have different numbers, but on average you should get at least three to five new referrals per year for each new patient. That means in a little over one year, those seven new clients would have paid for the direct-mail campaign sent out to attract them.

Over the years, what will those seven new clients be worth to you in additional business and referrals?

THE POWER OF HEADLINES

A few headline ideas to get your direct-marketing piece read, include:

- Your health is our business;

- A healthy life starts on the inside;

- Feel 10 years younger;

- When the pain just won't go away;

- Is it time for a personal tune-up?;

- Three reasons to give us a call today!;

- "I told my friends, I was used to the pain — I lied!";

- "My friends laughed when I told them I went to a back doctor, but then they saw me run for home plate."

Fritz Richard is the owner of MediaCrest, a company that deals with direct response marketing. He can be reached at 503-866-7419, MediaCrest@comcast.net, or through www.divineharvest.com.

Testamonials!

"Fritz's knowledge of marketing and sales has been fundamental in my plan to create a series of small seminars for local small business owners. Fritz has an ability to look beyond your basic marketing strategy and pull out best the benefits that will increase your potential return on investment."
Ron Seawood, Lead Generation Specialist, Redefined Marketing

"Fritz's direct mail campaigns are effective and reliable. Great, professional to work with."
Marlie Alberts, Freelance, Self Employed

"Fritz is a very outgoing creative individual that adapt to change. I know that he will do well with any opportunity presented to him. If you have additional questions, you may contact me."
Ken Johnson, Finance Manager, UPS

"Fritz is a very disciplined individual who takes every task seriously and does complete and respect time lines. He is also a pleasant person to work with and be around."
Keith Hunter, Worship Director, Mt. Olivet Baptist Church Portland, Oregon

"Fritz is a talented marketing executive that brings a fresh perspective to each project that I've worked with

him on. He does a great job of fully understanding the business goals and issues and providing creative marketing solutions that are geared to driving real accountable business results. He is also very easy to work with and is a great listener. His attention to detail is amazing. I have hired him for various projects and have been very pleased with him and his work."
Greg Johnson, Roots Marketing

"Fritz Richard is one of those rare, creative professionals that is an absolute joy to work with even on stiflingly, impossible deadlines. He has a talent for designing copy and graphics that effectively communicates and inspires action from a myriad of intended audiences."

Karin Tobiason, Principal, Karin Tobiason Public Relations

"Fritz has been very instrumental in solving very complex branding and creative challenges for my business. He masterfully combines exceptional creativity in practical ways that brings about real world solutions to real world problems. He immerses himself in the process and works hard to understand every aspect of the challenge and delivers a great product."

Rick Richard
CEO, Preenroll

"Fritz thought of the tagline that was a perfect complement to the logo and

the show. I chose one tagline out of about 10 that he presented. He was able to present me with a variety of taglines that exemplified the vision and content of the radio show.
Fritz is a true professional in every sense of the word. It was a pleasure working with him and I highly recommend his services."

Geoffrey C. Arnold
Spirit In Sports, Radio

"He is very committed and faithful in what he does. When he says he will help you he always follows through. He goes out of his way to make things happen and get stuff done."

Sharon Smith
Communication Coordinator

www.ingramcontent.com/pod-product-compliance
Lightning Source LLC
Chambersburg PA
CBHW061523180526
45171CB00001B/301